May we live without destruction
May we look to tomorrow with hope
May peace and light return to us

—*from "Oh Peace, Oh Light, Return,"*
from the movie Gojira *(1954)*

Wordsmith and podcaster, Warren Bluhm is a reporter, editor and storyteller who lives near the shores of Green Bay with his golden retrievers, Dejah and Summer.

BOOKS BY WARREN BLUHM

Author
Dejah & Summer in the Time of Magic
Ebenezer
It's Going to Be All Right
Echoes of Freedom Past
Full
Refuse to be Afraid
Gladness is Infectious
24 flashes
How to Play a Blue Guitar
Myke Phoenix: The Complete Novelettes
A Bridge at Crossroads
The Imaginary Revolution
A Scream of Consciousness
The Imaginary Bomb

Editor
Resistance to Civil Government – H.D. Thoreau
Letters to the Citizens of the United States – T. Paine
A Little Volume of Secrets
*The Haunted Bookshop – Christopher Morley
*Men at War – Andreas Latzko
*Trivia – Logan Pearsall Smith
*The Man Who Was Thursday – G.K. Chestrton
*The Demi-Gods – James Stephens
*The Story of My Heart – Richard Jefferies
* *The Roger Mifflin Collection*

a declaration of peace

Reflections on nonviolence

Warren Bluhm

warrenbluhm.com

A DECLARATION OF PEACE
Reflections on nonviolence
© 2024 Warren Bluhm. All rights reserved.
ISBN 979-8-9863331-9-9

Originally published as *War IS the Crime*.

Most of this book originally appeared on the website warrenbluhm.com, where the author blogs.

"Free people seek the light, always" also appears in the book *Full: Rockets, Bells & Poetry*.

This book is dedicated to all those who have served and sacrificed in times of war. Their heroism should never be questioned. The purpose here is to seek ways to honor their service by ensuring such sacrifice never again be needed.

"War is the health of the state."

— *Randolph Bourne*

"War is a racket."

— *General Smedley D. Butler*

TABLE OF CONTENTS

Preface	xi
Introduction: This book is about love	xv

PART 1: WAR IS THE CRIME

A silly little fairy tale	1
Imagine delegitimatizing war	4
'War Crime' is a redundant phrase	8
The economic foolishness of war	11
The most baffling, stupid and insane human activity	15
Seven O'Clock News/Silent Night	18
This week's war	21
Courtesy of 'our' former enemy	23
What a dream I had	26
Roger Mifflin and the truth about War	28
About those bioweapons	32
Revenge of the blind and the toothless	34
Mass murder as a political strategy	37

PART 2: A MISSION OF PEACE

I heard the Bells	45
A mission of peace	48
Peace, love and Godzilla	53
In praise of true detectives	59
On art and censorship	63
Peace, Nonviolence and Puppies	66
Puppies and world leaders	70
When they come in peace	71
Comfort while the storm rages	77
End the stupid	80
Maybe we can live as God intended	82
It starts with the first to say 'no'	85
The words must be there, somewhere	88
Free people seek the light, always	90
Good for nothing	93
Mother's Day Proclamation	95

PART 3: WHO WILL STAND FOR PEACE?

A way out of the mess	101
No more bullies	104
The goal of most sane humans	105

Memorial Day: No more wars	108
The greatest laws	109
We could get along if we wanted	112
A day for bridge building	114
There's a catch	116
Beatitudes	117
No time for hate	120
The myth of the masses	123
I am not your enemy	125
Wage peace	128
Will anyone stand for peace?	132
Author's note	135

Preface

There was a man who said, "Love the Lord Your God and Love Your Neighbor — those are the two most important things." They hung him on a cross to die.

There was a man who sat at a spinning wheel and taught how to win a revolution without violence. Someone shot him.

There was a president who reached out to his enemies for understanding instead of sending armies to kill them. Someone shot him.

There was a preacher who had a dream that his children would be judged on their character, not the color of their face. Someone shot him.

There was a musician who sang at the top of his lungs, "Give peace a chance." Someone shot him.

People want peace. People interact peacefully all day, every day. Everyone wants their children to grow up and live in peace. But it seems to be dangerous to say so.

Still, we have to keep saying it out loud until the psychopaths are overcome. War is a crime. People want to live in peace.

And shooting back is not the answer.

What we need

is

a declaration

of peace.

Introduction:
This book is about love

My life changed forever at 7:20 a.m. Tuesday, June 27, 2023. Or perhaps the real forever change happened on the day and time in July 1997 when I got an email from a woman who was trying to give away her box of vinyl records and saw in my America Online profile that I still collected them. That conversation led to other conversations, and we spent most of the next 26 years together.

Her nickname was Red. Her father's nickname was Big Red, her own flaming hair gave her the nickname Little Red, and when I wrote about her in my newspaper columns and later my blog posts, I called her just Red. I don't remember exactly when I realized she was the most beautiful woman I have ever known, but I was crazy about her.

That June 2023 moment was honestly the first time in my 70 years that I fully felt the loss that is death. I guess I'm a slow learner, or I needed someone that close to me to die before I understood.

Because she had been reconnecting with her faith as lymphoma began to take her life, and because long before the end she had asked me to read to her when the time came, I started reading parts of the Bible to my wife around 5:30 a.m. that day. I started with the Nativity story from Luke 2, detoured to Genesis 1, went through much of the Sermon on the Mount, and shared more Psalms than I remember. I made sure to include Proverbs 31 in the mix and was not surprised to realize that I was sitting next to the woman described in that passage.

After she passed away at about 7:20, I glanced at the laptop and found that I had been reading Matthew 22:34-40. I believe the last thing she heard on this mortal coil was:

And when the Pharisees heard that Jesus had silenced the Sadducees, they themselves gathered together. One of them, an expert in the law, tested

Him with a question: "Teacher, which commandment is the greatest in the Law?"

Jesus declared, "'Love the Lord your God with all your heart and with all your soul and with all your mind.' This is the first and greatest commandment. And the second is like it: 'Love your neighbor as yourself.' All the Law and the Prophets hang on these two commandments."

What wonderful words to share anytime, but especially at that particular moment!

People like to blame God for some of the most atrocious behavior humanity can produce, but scratch even slightly below the surface and you discover that the atrocities were committed not by God but by foolish humans who thoroughly misinterpreted the God whose two most important laws begin with the word "Love." It's not God's fault that we can't read or listen.

At a time like this, you realize how petty are our squabbles with our neighbors. Why waste time doing anything except loving when we have only a finite time on this planet?

It's been said that when an old person dies, a library burns. I feel that any death snuffs out a universe — years of experiences, decades of accumulated knowledge and wisdom.

John Lennon, among other folks, once said, "Life is what happens while you're busy making other plans." The Brave New Year of 2023 had barely begun when Red went into the hospital Jan. 3, beginning a journey that would end six months later on a hospice bed and changing all of my plans for the rest of my own life.

My outlook on the sanctity of life was altered by her journey, and I am flabbergasted more than ever by the prevailing culture's disdain for the value of human life. Our games and entertainment are rife with images of lives being casually eliminated, points awarded to the most prolific killers. No matter that each life represents years of painstaking education, growth and experience — a universe encased in every body.

Most dramatically this disdain for the value of

human life is exemplified by the institution of war. I have begun to burn with the belief that we must finally stop condoning war, which is nothing less than a notion that we can settle our differences by killing mass numbers of our adversaries. I started collecting some of those thoughts, the more recent reflections about peace and nonviolence as well as others I've written over the years. You are holding that collection now.

I have no illusions that I will sell many copies of this little book or that it will change the world in my lifetime, but I want to put these thoughts somewhere that they can be shared and, perhaps, taken to heart.

I truly believe I am not alone in these thoughts and that perhaps a book like this might encourage anyone who might be filled with despair because constant war seems inevitable. Constant war is nothing of the sort. People want peace, and we ought to be working together toward that goal.

As the bombs fall and the guns blaze somewhere in the world every day, it's easy to fear that we might never find a world where "Love your neighbor" is the prevailing philosophy. As I said, such a sea change is not likely to happen in this lifetime.

But I see how people mistreated each other in my youth — how institutions at one time treated whole groups of humans inhumanely — but those institutions began to change as people changed. Slowly, we have evolved.

And I realize that inch by inch, bird by bird, soul by soul, not all at once but slowly, the world has become a better place than it was one, 10, 50, and 100 years ago.

That is how war as an institution can eventually be abandoned — if you and I simply do what we can to make this day better than yesterday was, day by day.

Part 1
War IS The Crime

A silly little fairy tale

Once upon a time, there was a silly little kingdom and a silly little king. And one day another king came to visit and said silly things about the queen.

"How dare you!" cried the queen and slapped the visiting king.

"How dare you!" replied the visitor and went off in a huff.

"I am so offended!" said the silly little king, and he sent an army to go kill the visiting king.

But the visiting king had his own army, and instead of the king many minions died. The two armies killed many of each other, but the visiting king was never hurt.

One day the silly little king got a message. It

said: "You bloodsucker! You're going to have to do your own dirty work now. I'm still alive! You've managed to kill almost everyone else, but like a poor marksman you keep missing the target!"

This enraged the silly little king so much that he sent another army to ravage the other land and kill as many people as possible but especially the other king.

And the other king sent his own other army and the silly little kingdom was ravaged, too, but both kings stayed alive.

Years went by, and finally a peace conference was called.

"I hardly remember why we're fighting," said the silly little king. "We used to be friends, after all."

"I remember very well why we're fighting," said the other king. "The queen slapped me."

"Of course I did! You said silly things about me," said the queen.

"Yes, I recall that now," the other king said. "And I would do it again!"

"How dare you!" said the silly little king.

At that the peace conference ended, and to this day the two kingdoms are sending armies against one another, for all the good it does, which is no good at all.

You might say it's a silly thing to send many people to kill or be killed about, and you would be correct, but that's how these things happen.

The moral of the story is, well, there is no moral. There's nothing moral about war.

Imagine delegitimizing war

A deranged person goes into a public place with a gun and shoots as many innocents as possible in the time remaining before s/he is either apprehended or killed.

Deranged sociopaths in a safe place far, far away — those creatures we call politicians — condemn the shooter and discuss how weapons need to be removed from citizens' possession.

Nearly in the next sentence, and sometimes literally in the next sentence, the sociopaths discuss how many billions of dollars should be invested in sending people into public places and shooting as many innocents as possible — for what is war but a series of mass shooting incidents?

I pray for a world in which slaughter is universally condemned, whether committed by an insane person, at the behest of a government considered an adversary of our government, at the behest of a government considered a friend of our government, or especially at the behest of our government, since "our" government is supposedly the one we exert the most control over.

(I use the word "we" only for convenience's sake. I claim no ownership over the actions of the government that rules over my land. It takes actions every day that I neither condone nor support — but people are accustomed to saying "we" when they speak about that government, and so I use the pronoun, however incorrect and inappropriate it may be.)

I use the term "deranged sociopath" where it may be more genteel to say "politicians" or even "statesmen," because I see no difference between the insane person who shoots up a school or a grocery store and the insane person who advocates shooting up schools and stores in foreign lands, except that at least the active shooter does his own shooting rather than delegating the job to other people, which allows the politicians to pretend the death and destruction is an abstract concept.

Why do we — and this time "we" emphatically does not include me — continue to justify war as a legitimate way to settle our differences? That is the question that never gets asked. Never mind who shot first and who is shooting back in self-defense and what crime is being avenged. Why is killing as many adversaries as we can considered a legitimate way to settle our differences? It's a rhetorical question; I can't conceive of any justification for mass murder.

The innocent victim of war has just as many grieving parents and sisters and brothers as the victim of a random mass shooting. To the families of the victims, it doesn't matter whether it was an act of terrorism or an act of war — their loved ones are still gone and not coming back. No rhetoric can explain away their grief.

My point is simple: War *is not* a legitimate way to settle our differences. Raining death and destruction on another civilization is not a legitimate way to settle our differences. Violence is not a legitimate solution to our problems.

The sooner we delegitimize war in general — and the military-industrial complex specifically, all over the world — the sooner we approach the day when humanity lives in peace.

'War crime' is a redundant phrase

Reading the book *JFK and The Unspeakable: Why He Died and Why It Matters* by James W. Douglass, I am struck by the influence wielded by people who manufacture bombs and other implements to dismember people and destroy stuff. When Henry Kissinger died in December 2023, some folks grumbled about how he was a war criminal.

What is a "war crime," anyway? It seems to be defined as a crime against humanity that exceeds even the rules of conduct in a war zone. But what is a war if not a violation of civilization's rules of conduct?

War IS the crime. It's time to get past the notion that war is acceptable but certain behavior is unconscionable even in war. No: It's all unconscionable. We need to get to a place where it's generally agreed that killing as many of your adversaries as possible is an abomination.

Dwight Eisenhower's farewell address as president cautioned against the growing power of war profiteers and racketeers.

"In the councils of government, we must guard against the acquisition of undue influence, whether sought or unsought, by the military-industrial complex," said Eisenhower, a soldier who led the Allied military in the war against the Third Reich.

The world emerged from World War II weary of the struggle. The preamble to the United Nations Charter said as much: "We the peoples of the United Nations determined to save succeeding generations from the scourge of war, which twice in our lifetime has brought untold sorrow to mankind …"

But the war profiteers had other ideas, so here we are, 105 years after the War to End All Wars ended, 78 years after the end of World War II, and 63 years after Eisenhower's warning, still spending billions and trillions for killing on a horrifying scale.

One might conclude that by saying war is the crime, I am accusing the good men and women who have served in the armed forces of being criminals. Nothing could be further from the truth. They acted, often courageously, on the belief and culture that killing was appropriate in a time of war. They were and are creatures of that mindset. I am hammering at the foundation of that mindset.

I have friends and family who served, and I do not condemn their service. I do question the assumption that lies at the heart of it all, however, the assumption we were taught that mass killing is sometimes acceptable and unavoidable. We will probably not make progress as a species until we change that assumption. But I cannot condemn centuries of soldiers and other military personnel who believed there was no other way.

The economic foolishness of war

Not long ago I was introduced to a fascinating 2022 article by historian H.A. Scott Trask titled "[Ten Recurring Economic Fallacies, 1774-2004](#)," on the Mises Institute website. Trask identified 10 mistakes that government, corporate and academic leaders have made over and over again over the more than two centuries that the U.S. of A. has been the U.S. of A.

It is no surprise today that the first three of the fallacies have to do with those leaders' attitude toward the most economically devastating of all human endeavors: War. For some reason they keep rationalizing that war is somehow a net economic good.

Myth #1 is the idea that when someone breaks a

window, it's actually a boost to the economy: a window manufacturer gets an order, a hardware store sells a new window, a carpenter is hired to install it — in other words, money circulates and job are created all around.

"The fallacy lies in a failure to grasp what has been foregone by repair and reconstruction—the labor and capital expended, having been lost to new production," Trask writes.

He chides the economists who argued that the government's response to the horrific 9/11 attack would lift the country out of recession.

"What was never mentioned was that resources devoted to repair, security, and war-fighting are resources that cannot be devoted to creating consumer goods, building new infrastructure, or enhancing our civilization," says Trask.

Myth #2 is that war is good for the economy. This fallacy is often cited by people who believe it was World War II, not FDR's New Deal, that ultimately lifted the U.S. out of the Great Depression.

"The truth is that war, and the preparation for it, is economically wasteful and destructive. Apart from the spoils gained by winning (if it is won) war and defense spending squander labor, resources, and wealth, leaving the country poorer in the end than if these things had been devoted to peaceful endeavors," Trask writes. "During war, the productive powers of a country are diverted to producing weapons and ammunition, transporting armaments and supplies, and supporting the armies in the field."

He quotes William Graham Sumner, who lived through the U.S. Civil War: "The mills, forges, and factories were active in working for the government, while the men who ate the grain and wore the clothing were active in destroying, and not in creating capital. This, to be sure, was war. It is what war means, but it cannot bring prosperity."

Trask's Myth #3 applies only tangentially to war — the fallacy that the best way to finance a war is by borrowing. I say it's tangential because borrowing is the worst way to finance just about anything —

whenever you "buy now, pay later," you end up spending exponentially more money than the purchase price. But going into debt to pay for a war is exponentially more foolish as going to war in the first place.

War is a gigantic waste in terms of human lives lost and forever altered, infrastructure destroyed, and economic bankruptcy — not to mention moral bankruptcy. As Isaac Asimov wrote in his novel *Foundation*, "Violence is the last refuge of the incompetent. It is the only resort by which incompetent men can thrive. The bully, the brute, the dictator."

Trask's article is educational reading for anyone interested in how leaders continue to misstep as they attempt to mess in economic affairs, but especially for anyone who seriously believes there could be an economic benefit to going to war. The only economic benefit is lining the pockets of war profiteers, a benefit that hardly balances war's astronomical costs.

The most baffling, stupid and insane human activity

The human body is a remarkable instrument, as you surely know if you ever pay any attention to yours.

Sometimes I sit and consider my heart, which has been beating regularly nonstop for more than 70 years, and my lungs, which inflate and deflate more or less automatically, and the whole system that reprocesses the food I eat and the other things this body does, not to mention this bio-electric device inside my skull that makes it all work, and I am in awe.

It helps me respect the other people I encounter all the time, whose bodies and minds are just as miraculous.

I am gobsmacked by some of those people,

though, particularly the ones who develop ways to rip, tear, shred and disintegrate bodies and minds, and most especially the ones who invent reasons to use those weapons.

War is the most baffling, stupid and insane human activity ever invented. If the intent is to resolve a difference of opinion, it's also useless. How many Ukrainians do you imagine have been convinced that their land really belongs to Russia, as a result of being bombed for the cause? How many Afghans lost loved ones to U.S. weaponry and concluded, yep, those Americans were right all along? All the violence does is perpetuate the violence in an endless cycle of revenge and retribution.

All of those war victims lived inside human bodies as miraculous as the one you're occupying this very moment. Can you imagine the depravity it takes to order such destruction by the thousand?

I'm not talking about the soldiers caught up in the system and fighting for their lives; I'm talking about the sociopaths who sit in safe little rooms and say, "I'm mad at that sociopath in another safe little room miles away from here, so let's you go kill people and blow up stuff in his country!"

Somebody has to say no to these madmen. Just no, no more. We ain't gonna study war no more, except as a classroom exercise about why ceding authority to sociopaths is always a bad idea.

They say war is hell, and I say to hell with war. Lay down the weapons, beat them into plowshares, and the next time someone suggests going to war or supporting a war, tell them to STFU.

Seven O'clock News/ Silent Night

Good morning and welcome to the news. We have a remarkable list of terrible things that humans have done to each other over the last 24 hours or so, for your entertainment.

Four people were killed and several others wounded when an angry young man with a gun opened fire on a crowd of people 573 miles from here. Look at this video — we must warn you, some people may find this video disturbing, but you should look. Go ahead, you can handle it.

Here's a conversation with the leader of a group that says the latest gun deaths are another example of why people should not be entrusted with weapons to defend themselves from personal attack.

Here in our hometown, a person got drunk and rolled her car down an embankment. She later died of her injuries at a local hospital.

Overseas, the death toll is now in the tens of thousands from that war that has been going on for nearly two years, and things are just as bleak in the new war. In Washington, debate is underway over whether the U.S. should send millions, billions or trillions of dollars worth of weaponry to the two war zones to ensure that the killing is safe, effective, ongoing, and benefits our preferred warlords.

People are homeless and starving after a natural disaster a few states over from here, and one political party is chastising the other for not voting in favor of more federal government spending in the disaster zone. The main point of contention is whether to raise the debt ceiling again to pay for it all.

After the break, a special report about ways the government is working to protect innocent humans from the ravages that the government wrought in their lives in the first place. And folks around here are bracing for cold; we'll tell you why.

But first, a selection of messages about magic pills that adjust the chemical composition of your body to make you healthier, wealthier, and wiser. You won't want to miss this.

This week's war

So another war is thrust into our consciousness and sides are chosen. There is our side and the wrong side and how dare you?

More indiscriminate slaughter of innocents who have no dispute with you — why? What is the point of all this? Where does it end? WHEN does it end?

The only winners are the weapons makers who profit from haters buying their wares. Everyone dies, but the manufacturers feed their families. What a business: Build things that are designed to destroy themselves and anyone in their path, and so there is an endless need to replenish the supply.

I am on the side that beats swords into plowshares, the side with a God who declares we should love one another including our supposed enemies.

I remember a meme from my youth, before memes were called memes: "What if they gave a war and nobody came?" We're still waiting for the answer, because eager young people still flock to join the new war, and the rest of us root from the sidelines, offering money, weapons, aid and comfort to the killers.

Please don't ask me to take sides or declare my solidarity. I stand with the peacemakers. I stand with anyone and everyone who shouts, "Enough is enough." I stand with anyone who, upon hearing that they're giving a war, refuses to come.

Courtesy of 'our' former enemy

As I write this particular reflection, I am on Page 219 of this 240-page journal, my 22nd, so I probably will have all the pages filled by the end of the year. I have already purchased the book that I plan to use for Journal #23. It is a blue-covered version of this Threshold-brand journal from Target. It's a serviceable little book, essentially as good as a Moleskine at half the price. I could probably go even cheaper, but the craftsmen/women who make these books deserve to make a few coins for their effort.

The notice on the back label says "Origin: Vietnam. © 2023 Target Books." They have copyrighted the venue — the pen scratchings inside are © 2023 Warren Bluhm, I would hope. I own the words and the drawings and any detectable melody.

Theoretically, I own myself and this pudgy, worn wreck of a body that I have inhabited for going on 71 years. I am not the best possible steward of this body, but neither it nor I had any choice in this relationship.

It's a bit ironic that the book was created in Vietnam, since the government in this part of the world spent many years blowing up people and things in that part of the world over ideological differences, and now here we are exchanging goods and services like normal human beings without a serious quarrel with each other.

It's sad that we "needed" to go through that hellacious ordeal in order to reach this state of normalcy.

Many people sincerely believe war can be a necessary evil in settling our differences.

Someone has lied to them. Somewhere, someone is teaching that lie.

War is evil — not a necessary evil, just evil.

War is a waste.

War is a crime.

Are "war crimes" any worse than the idea of war itself?

No, war itself is the crime.

What a dream I had

There's the signpost up ahead — We're entering the zone where not much can be explained rationally. How do such things happen? Only through explanations beyond the grasp of the average human. Of course, what is "average" anyway, and for that matter what is "human"?

We have all been dropped into a giant prank show, or perhaps a giant psy-op if you prefer sinister motives. "What can I get away with today?" asked the sociopath in charge, and he directed his minions to give his latest experiment a try.

Oh wait, I just woke up a few minutes ago. I thought I was watching the morning news, but it was all a bad dream, wasn't it? I was still asleep. There aren't really people out there acting as if the government ruled us instead of the other way around. There aren't really people who are mixed up about what "by the people, of the people, for the people" means. I was just having a nightmare, and freedom of speech is still rocking and rolling, and no one is abusing freedom of the press to the point where the press is a parody of itself. What a dream I had! I'm glad I was asleep and all that goofy stuff wasn't really coming down.

It was weird, though — up was down, good was evil, in was out, freedom was slavery, and ignorance was strength. The scariest part was when people started talking as if war was peace, as if peace was abnormal and kindness was a weakness. The lunatics were in charge of the proverbial asylum, and if you noticed, you were accused of being a lunatic yourself or a dupe of a foreign power.

Phew! The dream felt so real I didn't realize I was dreaming.

Roger Mifflin and the truth about War

One of my favorite books is an obscure novel written more than a century ago in the aftermath of The Great War. Christopher Morley wrote *The Haunted Bookshop* in 1919 as a sequel to his first book, *Pernassus on Wheels*. Both books follow the adventures of Roger Mifflin, a feisty bookseller who believed in the power of the written word and made it his mission to match people with the books they need most.

In this second book Mifflin has retired the horse and wagon he had been using to peddle his volumes and instead opened a bricks-and-mortar bookstore with his beloved wife, Helen. He has agreed to take in a friend's daughter, Titania, and in this scene Mifflin rails about the horrors of war and how government leaders censored the truth about what was happening to boys in the trenches.

The book, and this scene, struck home with me, because it seems not much has changed in 100 years.

+ + + + +

"Sometimes I thought Truth had vanished from the earth," he cried bitterly. "Like everything else, it was rationed by the governments. I taught myself to disbelieve half of what I read in the papers. I saw the world clawing itself to shreds in blind rage. I saw hardly any one brave enough to face the brutalizing absurdity as it really was, and describe it. I saw the glutton, the idler, and the fool applauding, while brave and simple men walked in the horrors of hell. The stay-at-home poets turned it to pretty lyrics of glory and sacrifice. Perhaps half a dozen of them have told the truth. Have you read Sassoon? Or Latzko's *Men in War*, which was so damned true that the government suppressed it? Humph! Putting Truth on rations!"

He knocked out his pipe against his heel, and his

blue eyes shone with a kind of desperate earnestness.

"But I tell you, the world is going to have the truth about War. We're going to put an end to this madness. It's not going to be easy. Just now, in the intoxication of the German collapse, we're all rejoicing in our new happiness. I tell you, the real Peace will be a long time coming. When you tear up all the fibres of civilization it's a slow job to knit things together again. You see those children going down the street to school? Peace lies in their hands. When they are taught in school that war is the most loathsome scourge humanity is subject to, that it smirches and fouls every lovely occupation of the mortal spirit, then there may be some hope for the future. But I'd like to bet they are having it drilled into them that war is a glorious and noble sacrifice.

"The people who write poems about the divine frenzy of going over the top are usually those who dipped their pens a long, long way from the slimy duckboards of the trenches. It's funny how we hate to face realities. I knew a commuter once who rode in town every day on the 8:13. But he used to call it the 7:73. He said it made him feel more virtuous."

There was a pause, while Roger watched some belated urchins hurrying toward school.

"I think any man would be a traitor to humanity who didn't pledge every effort of his waking life to an attempt to make war impossible in future."

About those bioweapons

There was a time when you risked being called a racist or a Russian stooge if you believed the COVID-19 virus could have escaped from a laboratory in Wuhan, China. A few years later, it turns out you just had your eyes open.

In all of the discussion, I don't recall any discussion about the main question I would ask about that lab.

Why? Why does it exist?

Why is anyone studying "gain of function" virology — that is to say, why is anyone studying ways to make viruses more deadly? What monsters would weaponize disease?

Life is short and often cruel. Why study how to make it shorter and crueler?

I'm relieved that people have finally come to their senses enough to realize that if a pandemic has its roots in the same town as a bioweapons laboratory, the lab might have had something to do with it.

But I'm discouraged by the thought that someone took leave of their senses and convinced enough other people to build and equip a place where diseases are stored against the day when they can be deployed against human beings.

I have no illusions "they" are the only ones conducting such studies. I am fully confident that "we" operate a bunch of these hellish laboratories "ourselves."

The quotation marks are because I don't believe such insanity belongs either to "us" or to "them." Normal people don't think or behave like the sociopaths who claim to rule us.

Someday, I hope and pray, humans will be better than this.

Revenge of the blind and the toothless

Friday afternoon, Feb. 2, 2024, as folks were turning off their brains for the weekend including the alleged Washington press corps, the U.S. military and the White House released statements that were repeated more or less verbatim in what passed for news coverage of the event.

U.S. Central Command announced that it blew up a bunch of people in Iraq and Syria, striking 85 targets using "more than 125 precision munitions." As of Sunday morning, 18 people were confirmed dead.

The attack was described as retaliation for a Jan. 28 assault that killed three U.S. soldiers and wounded about 40 other people at a military base in Jordan near its border with Syria, according to a statement from whoever is running the U.S. government using Joe Biden's name.

"Our response begins today. It will continue at times and places of our choosing," the statement said.

After that ominous promise, the very next words of the statement were, "The United States does not seek conflict in the Middle East or anywhere else in the world."

If this is the U.S. government not seeking conflict, I shudder to think what seeking conflict looks like.

Once again a mass murder is met by mass murder on a grander scale. The word is that the people in Iraq and Syria are planning their own retaliation, and of course the U.S. government has already promised that it's not finished. And the cycle of violence goes ever onward.

When a deranged individual commits mass murder, political deflectors always call for new laws restricting potential victims' access to weapons of self-defense. Where are these political animals when mass murder is committed in the name of governments?

The slaughter will continue until civilized humans refuse to accept mass murder as a legitimate method of settling our differences. The big question is who will be the first to beat swords into plowshares?

The old saw is that if you follow "an eye for an eye, a tooth for a tooth to its logical conclusion, the combatants eventually will all be blind and toothless.

And in the meantime, more names are added to the legions of grieving families and friends, more dreams are added to the list of hopes that will never come true, and more despair is heaped on the notion that humans can ever live in peace.

Mass murder as a political strategy

Humans have waged war against each other since the beginning of time, but that does not change the fact that war is a crime against humanity — murder and destruction on a massive scale.

Ah, but what about the "good" wars? The Revolutionary War that secured independence from King George III and gave us the Declaration of Independence and the Bill of Rights? The Civil War that ended slavery? World War II that slapped down the Third Reich?

Violence begets violence. A revolution replaces one regime with another, sometimes a less brutal one as in 1783, sometimes more brutal as in Russia in 1917. Meet the new boss, same as the old boss. World War II ended Hitler, but his mad concept of superior and inferior races lingers on. Even after a Civil War that freed the slaves, slavery exists in other forms, and the foolish belief that some people are lesser beings because of their skin color has never been eradicated as it should be.

What those wars did accomplish was to cut thousands of lives short, lives that could have cured cancer or inspired millions or finally found a way for us to live in peace.

Is it simply human nature to want to lash out and extinguish the lives of people who have wronged us in one way or another? Perhaps it is — rage is a real and terrible force. But returning rage with rage, an eye for an eye, does not repair the injury or bring back the dead. If anything, it only continues the cycle of violence.

The only "good" that a war might do is if the actual goal is to "reduce the surplus population," as Dickens put it. And even at that, war is a horribly inefficient tool, taking the strong with the weak, the best and brightest in equal measure with the worst and darkest. I think we should be wary when people who believe the planet can't support this many humans start talking about the need to wage war against this country or that country. One might suspect it's not about ideology or freedom or democracy as much as it's about indiscriminate killing.

The idea of civilization is to rein in the more beastly impulses of human nature. The rules are simple — don't steal, don't kill, don't commit violence to get your way. War is often seen as the opposite of civilization, because it is exactly that — combatants are told their duty is to commit lethal acts against other human beings with whom they have no personal quarrel and could even be friends in a more civilized setting.

I keep coming back to the gentle man from Galilee who preached forgiveness and said the two most important laws are to love God and love your enemy, and even love your enemy. People who deny he was nonviolent sometimes note that he overturned the tables in the temple — but he didn't slaughter the people manning those tables.

If Jesus had armed his 12 apostles and used them to assemble an army to kill as many people as possible until the Roman Empire was defeated, well, I'm certain we might remember him as a historical figure but we wouldn't worship him. Instead, he taught us to turn the other cheek, and human nature being what it is, the great saints are remembered as martyrs, like Steven who was stoned to death for preaching the gospel.

We don't know the names of anyone who picked up a stone that day, not even the first coward to hurl a rock, and their lives are forgotten in the ashes of history. But Steven's name and his words live on, and in that fact is the ultimate defeat of war and other violence: No matter how many people you slaughter for speaking the truth, the truth will still ring true, and all the killing will bear no fruit.

Returning evil with evil only perpetuates evil. The enemy you slay will never have a chance to get to know you and become your friend. If he's trying to kill you, defend yourself. But participate in a manufactured scenario where the rules are kill or be killed? Madness!

War is the last resort of scoundrels who can't make peace with their neighbors. Does it matter who started it? Evil is evil, and one of the sacred commandments is "Do not murder." Even atheists outlaw murder. It's time we found alternatives to mass murder for resolving our conflicts.

Do I have a grand strategy for ending war? No. All I have is an individual desire to live in peace with other humans, to treat them with respect and, yes, love, and to understand that other individual humans are as worthy of life as I think I am, and I should let them live their lives as they see fit as long as they respect other people's right to be left alone in peace. Perhaps we can convince and transform one another one heart at a time.

A long time somebody asked the rhetorical question, "What if they gave a war and nobody came?" My hope and prayer is, one day, enough hearts will be convinced and transformed for that to become real.

Part 2

A Mission of Peace

44 A DECLARATION OF PEACE

I Heard the Bells

After one particularly lovely Christmas weekend with family and rest and recharging, and as I contemplated going back to work, a sort of melancholy settled over me.

I found myself thinking of the Henry Wadsworth Longfellow poem that was reworked into a Christmas carol, "I Heard the Bells on Christmas Day." Longfellow wrote the poem in 1863 during the U.S. Civil War, and despite its optimistic conclusion, the poem's penultimate stanza remains the money quote:

And in despair I bowed my head;
"There is no peace on earth," I said;
"For hate is strong,
And mocks the song
Of peace on earth, good-will to men!"

In the final stanza, Longfellow asserts that the living God will see to it that "The Wrong shall fail, the Right prevail, with peace on earth, good-will to men." But 160 years after it was written, hate is still strong and still mocks the call for peace.

Sometime between Nov. 1 and Thanksgiving Day, the air becomes filled with the familiar songs of the season, singing joy to the world and tidings of comfort and joy. Come Dec. 26 the songs are all packed away and forgotten, and we go back to the nihilism and back-biting and hate-thy-neighbor norm.

And there's the reason for my melancholy: I'd so much rather press for peace and good-will on earth, and it's frustrating to see how much power is wielded by the forces who prefer to see us at each other's throats.

One of these days it would be lovely to see people rise up and just say "no" to the bottom feeders who spend their days building weapons to kill as many people as possible in one fell swoop, who concoct arguments to convince us that certain people deserve to have those weapons trained against them, and who stand by silently while the hate mongers rage away.

How many "nos" will it take to achieve peace on earth? I say we try to find out.

A mission of peace

In the first few days of the new year, my thoughts on war and peace began coalescing, and I concluded that it's time "Peace on Earth" became something more than pretty words devoid of real meaning, an empty phrase we mouth at Christmastime but never actually consider as a realistic goal.

I am here, and I assembled this book, on a mission of peace — nonviolent resistance to the war machine.

Enough of sundered bodies and crumbled cities. We must learn to love one another. We must learn to live in peace with our neighbors and understand that *all* humans are our neighbors.

We need not be friends, although we may find

we have more in common than we realize. We can at least be neighbors.

We owe it to the spirit of life to be kind to each other. We will all be dead soon enough; why not live — and let live — while we're here? It's our debt to the fallen and the lost: We survived for a reason, and the reason begins with living.

I am angry — yes, I think "angry" says it best — at the idea that some people spend their careers inventing ingenious new implements to kill other people. Life is such a precious gift, and nature snatches it away from us so soon as it is. How dare we manufacture the means to speed the process?

I have no quarrel so deep that it merits taking the life of the one with whom I quarrel. Even an evil person who takes other lives — What good is accomplished by duplicating his crime and taking his life?

I am angry with the one who takes an eye, and I am angry with the one who takes an eye for an eye and by doing so continues the seemingly endless cycle of violence. Who will be the first to say "enough"? Who will refuse to commit war?

Do even I have the will to refuse? If violence is committed or threatened against me, will I have the courage to say, "No more of this, I don't know if I can forgive you, but I will not respond in kind"? Am I defying human nature itself to suggest such a reaction?

Now that I have gone through the death of my closest loved one, I am loathe to visit this depth of loss on another human being. Death visits us all; let us not be in a hurry, especially with regard to other people's lives. As the song says, and I know I repeat myself now, "Only God has the right to decide who'a to live and die."

The character in an "action" movie says, "Let's kill them all and let God sort it out." The statement itself acknowledges that the sorting is not our job, and if it isn't, then neither is it our job to do the killing.

Death comes soon enough, let's not hurry the process. Our duty, our mission, our purpose, is to live. Our obligation is to life — our best possible life.

We have no right to take life or to delegate the taking of life to some monstrous entity or collective.

Now that we've settled that, what is this "life" of which I speak? As I said at the outset, in my belief we have two laws to live by — it all boils down to Love God and Love Your Neighbor, and even then people quibble over these simple laws. "Who or what is God?" The creator of the universe and all we see, an awesome and diverse creation beyond our meager imagination. The idea is to love this something or someone greater than all of us — the something or someone who created all of this.

Dozens of birds are feeding on our back deck as I write, each of them a miraculous creation, pecking at seeds each of which is in itself a miraculous creation. Within my limited line of sight are thousands if not millions of miraculous creations, and there are billions of creatures like me on this planet each of us witnessing thousands of miracles, and this planet is one of an infinite number of planets in this universe. Of course I love the Creator. At the very least I am in awe of the beauty and vastness of creation.

And who is my neighbor? The person who lives one house over? The person sitting next to me? If I may be so bold, when considered in the context of a universe, every one of those billions of creatures like me is "sitting next to me." I am obligated to love my neighbor, all 8 billion of them.

It's an exhausting thought, the idea of loving every person I encounter, so exhausting that it's hard to stay angry. The only energy worth generating, in the end, is love.

And so live and love. Live in love. It feels like the healthiest way to live. As I reach that conclusion, I seem to feel a weight lifting off my shoulders, and I see a road to life.

Peace, love and Godzilla

I love movies, but even I am rarely affected by a film as deeply as I was by *Godzilla Minus One*, written and directed by Takashi Yamazaki. It's probably the most unexpectedly moving film I've ever seen. (There is a spoiler or two ahead; I warned ya.)

The story is set in the closing days of World War II and the years just afterward. Even more literally than in the original 1954 film *Gojira*, *Godzilla Minus One* is about Japan's recovery from that devastating war.

The war, as war is wont to do, has crushed the spirit of many a Japanese person, and they struggle to emerge from the devastation. Then, as they begin the long, slow recovery, they must deal with a giant radioactive creature that knocks them back down again — if the war left them with zero, now they are at minus-one.

Still, we meet people who refuse to surrender to despair. One is a woman named Noriko, who is caring for a child whose parents were killed in the bombing of Tokyo. She finds shelter with our central protagonist, Koichi, a shell-shocked pilot still haunted by decisions he made during the war. Before she is swept away by Godzilla's atomic breath, Noriko tells Koichi that those who survived the war have an obligation to live; they are "meant to live," she says.

Noriko's challenge to Koichi is to get past his demons and make something of life, to live in gratitude for and in honor of those who perished. It's a life-affirming moment in what ultimately is a life-affirming story.

The film probably affected me more deeply because of the emotional devastation I experienced after Red's death. I will not insult the victims of war by equating my suffering with theirs, but I realize this single personal experience with death is surely multiplied in a war zone to a degree beyond my imagination.

I can't help but recommend this film to everyone, even many people with a distaste for monster movies in general. At some point in all our lives, we need to hear about this obligation to live and keep going in the face of unspeakable loss, and I have an inkling that's why the film seems to resonate with so many people.

Its unrelenting commitment to hope and life is, as I said, as unexpectedly moving as any film I've ever seen. I mean, come on, who goes to a Godzilla movie expecting to be moved to tears? I am not the first to declare that Yamazaki has created a masterpiece that transcends its genre and delivers an anti-war tale for the ages.

+ + + + +

As I was anticipating the U.S. release of *Godzilla Minus One*, I took another of my occasional looks at the film that started it all, the 1954 Japanese classic *Gojira,* and was again struck by what an awesome film it is and still so relevant in this crazy world of ours.

The crux of the film is convincing research scientist Dr. Serizawa to employ the horrible weapon he accidentally discovered to kill the 150-meter-tall monster that has ravaged Tokyo — an ancient dinosaur made even more dangerous due to the radiation from H-bomb tests in the Pacific.

Serizawa is convinced his device — the oxygen destroyer — must remain a secret for humanity's sake.

"If the oxygen destroyer is used even once, politicians from around the world will see it. Of course, they'll want to use it as a weapon," Serizawa explains. "Bombs vs. bombs, missiles vs. missiles, and now a new super weapon to throw upon us all! As a scientist — no, as human being, I can't allow that to happen."

He is finally convinced by the televised images of the ruined Tokyo and a girls choir singing a mournful prayer for peace called "Oh Peace, Oh Light, Return":

May we live without destruction
May we look to tomorrow with hope
May peace and light return to us

But Serizawa insists on operating the oxygen destroyer himself, burns all his notes, and after deploying the underwater weapon that destroys the giant monster, he cuts the hose linking him to the surface, choosing to die rather than to risk being coerced to share the secrets of the horrible device.

As the story closes, Professor Yamane, who has served in the role of the scientist who wants to study Godzilla, not destroy him, says, "I can't believe that Godzilla was the only surviving members of its species, but if we keep on conducting nuclear tests, it's possible that another Godzilla might appear, somewhere in the world, again."

The film ends with a reprise of the prayer for peace.

The story was sanitized when *Gojira* was recut for American audiences and titled *Godzilla, King of the Monsters*. Serizawa's on-target description of political animals was edited and dampened. The words of the hymn were never shared, leaving only its mournful tone. And, of course, Yamane's warning that we should stop testing nuclear weapons was nowhere to be heard.

In fact, the original Japanese version of the film was impossible to find in the U.S. outside of bootleg editions. I was one of the first in line to buy the DVD when it finally was released in America in 2004, the 50th anniversary of the movie.

Godzilla, King of the Monsters was one of the formative movies of my childhood, fueling my love of science fiction and the fantastic, but I was thunderstruck upon seeing the film its creators intended.

Its message, nine years after Hiroshima and Nagasaki, is simple and powerful: May we live without destruction; may we look to tomorrow with hope. That U.S. citizens were not allowed to see that film for 50 years speaks volumes.

In praise of true detectives

I think I've finally realized why I like murder mysteries so much.

My mother adored Hercule Poirot and Perry Mason. Whenever she might be caught reading a book, you could bet Agatha Christie or Erle Stanley Gardner would be the author. I inherited her delight in the Belgian detective but have concluded that the invincible defense attorney is an acquired taste.

Incited by well-done television adaptations, I have found myself racing through the adventures of Harry Bosch, Walt Longmire, Cork O'Connor, Inspector Banks, and a few other current and former law officers who track down killers. And while Mason's appeal as a defense attorney escapes me, I have relished every case that Mickey Haller and Andy Carpenter have tackled.

I have averaged consuming 84 books annually for the past six years, most of them audiobooks as I commute or otherwise cruise around northeast Wisconsin. That's more than 500 books, and I would guess at least 200 of them have been murder mysteries.

Why? As I've been focusing in recent days about our culture of death and glorification of the exercise in mass murder called war, I thought about my appetite for detective and crime stories — what is their appeal to me? I drew three conclusions.

1. Among all genres of popular fiction, murder mysteries generally feature only one violent death, or perhaps a second or third as the killer fears discovery and seeks to cover up the original crime.

2. Each death is treated as an affront and an aberration.

3. And the goal is to apprehend and punish the killer, and preferably by putting him or her behind bars. A killer's death is often depicted as an escape

from justice.

Contrast this with typical behaviors in other mass entertainment. I am following the latest season of the TV show *Reacher*, and this week's episode ended with a kill-or-be-killed showdown that claimed the fictional lives of three henchmen, but the mastermind got away to fight another episode or two. This was a defeat for the title character, who earlier in the episode had casually said of the bad guy, "We're going to find him and kill him."

Life is casually extinguished in these shows, usually in violent ways and as spectacularly as the writers can imagine. Is it any wonder why, out here in the world of non-fiction, so much violent death is condoned or even celebrated?

Harry Bosch's creed, oft quoted when he's asked why he's trying so hard to find the murderer of some low-life, is "Everyone matters or nobody matters." Reacher's creed is "We're going to find him and kill him." That may be the essence of why I prefer murder mysteries to "action" thrillers and the like.

The death of a single human being erases a lifetime of experiences, an entire universe of insights and interactions and contributions to the human adventure. When a person dies, the world is diminished. This is the central premise of the murder mystery: The deliberate taking of a life is a tragedy and a crime.

And that, I think, is why I like to read murder mysteries.

On art and censorship

I have Folk Alley in the background this morning. It's a streaming service that offers traditional and modern folk music 24/7. Music is an improvement over predawn silence or the litany of woes, tribulation, evil and unhappiness that comprises the TV news most mornings.

We choose every day whether to dwell on death or to dwell on life. Both forces roam the earth in equal portions, but only life offers hope and redemption and a tomorrow.

The musicians explore beauty and the rhythms of life — sometimes they experiment with discord, but even then they are seeking patterns and beauty in odd nooks and crannies. There is an order to things, and artists shine lights on that order in new and surprising ways, and also old and familiar ways.

Art — poetry, music, imagery — is a uniquely human thing, arranging sounds and images in delightful ways to bring a smile and a surge of emotion.

"I didn't mean to make you cry" — Oh, but I did, the purging relief of tears, the exhalation of laughter, the emotion of it all, the awe and the joy — I was hoping to bottle it for you to relive and rediscover in the times when you need it again.

And so this is art — an attempt to capture a feeling to be tapped as needed over and over, the past reassuring the future that a time came when all was well, and it can be again.

("For Emily, Wherever I May Find Her" came across the Folk Alley feed just then, two minutes of sheer beauty and exactly the reassurance I was writing about.)

The words and music relay ancient emotions snatched from the heart of yes, reassurance, peace, and hope for a better future.

Why would someone want to remove such aspirations from anyone? Tyrants are puzzling creatures: Once they were children with innocent questions and open minds and hearts, and along the way they found answers in oppressing and leashing their neighbors.

I wonder how they found those answers. I wonder if they realize they are tyrants. Don't each of us aspire to the best in us? How do you find the best by chaining us? Only by flying free do you discover the view from the sky.

Peace, Nonviolence and Puppies

I was going through an exercise in Bob Goff's book *Dream Big* and, in response to the prompt "Are there some recurring themes in your behaviors and choices?" I wrote in all-caps, "PEACE. NONVIOLENCE. PUPPIES."

I realized then that he may have been talking more about behaviors I want to adjust as opposed to themes that I often return to in my thoughts and writings, but those really are three of my "passion topics."

I really can't think of a human activity more downright foolish than war. People — or more accurately their leaders or rulers — have a disagreement, and to resolve their differences they hurl their subjects at each other with a goal of killing as many of their opponents' subjects as possible. That resolves nothing: Everyone still disagrees, and the only real results are resentment, grief, anger and a greater hatred than existed before the killing started.

My experience is that people want peace. Almost every transaction and interaction between humans is peaceful. War is an aberration and represents nothing by the most utter failure to keep the peace, which supposedly is the principal purpose of government. I started out confused by the whole concept, and I have become more virulently anti-war as time goes on.

Losing Red, the wonderful human being with whom I shared the last quarter century, has made me even more so. Hers was a peaceful death — or as peaceful a death as a horrible disease can offer — but the loss has helped me understand, in a way I hadn't quite grasped before, just how devastating and complete death is. To cause the premature death of another human being, deliberately, is nothing short of insane.

I have written often of my admiration for

Mohandas Gandhi, Martin Luther King Jr., and Jesus the Christ, with regard to their commitment to nonviolent solutions.

"Love your enemies, do good to those who hate you, bless those who curse you, pray for those who mistreat you," Jesus said. "If someone strikes you on one cheek, turn to him the other also. And if someone takes your cloak, do not withhold your tunic as well." That's hard advice to swallow, but it's more likely to turn an enemy into a friend someday than killing that enemy and as many of his friends as you can.

And then there's puppies. Do I really need to say more? There are dozens if not hundreds of writings and memes about how if you want to learn about unconditional love, pay attention to your puppy. The bond between puppy and human is one of the greatest examples to follow about how to love.

I was going to write "One of the greatest examples to follow about how to love your neighbor," but a puppy can get pretty feisty if a neighbor or other stranger is perceived as a threat to those she loves. In the absence of a threat, though, there's nothing like puppy love. If turning the other cheek doesn't work, try handing your enemy a puppy.

Puppies and world leaders

There is more love in a puppy's eyes than in any president's.

There is more trust in an old dog's eyes than in those of any king, queen, prime minister or chancellor.

There is more heart in a hound than in any sociopath who wants to be master.

Yes, I trust my dog more than any government leader. So if my dog doesn't like you, I'm not so sure I should, either.

When they come in peace

I love, love, love movies with mysterious aliens who turn out to have our best interests at heart — movies where the "villain" is our human fear of the unknown and the impulse to destroy what we don't understand.

We need more stories like that.

The aliens come in peace, and our instinct is to strike. When our ape ancestor discovers tools in *2001*, he goes within seconds from simple work to hunting and then to killing his enemy — the urge to weaponize our discoveries is strong within us, but as we grow we put away childish urges and impulses — don't we?

I love when the strange and mysterious adversary becomes our best friend, or at least an ally, because we've all been strange and mysterious to someone at some time or another in our lives, or we've taken a chance to be nice to a mysterious stranger or newcomer who ends up being our best friend for life.

It makes more sense to believe the aliens come in peace, because we come in peace every day, in almost every interaction with others.

My favorite of the *Star Trek: The Next Generation* movies is easily *First Contact*.

In the Trek mythology, the Vulcans discovered Earth on the day Zefram Cochrane performed a successful warp drive experiment. A passing Vulcan craft detected the warp drive signature — a sign of an advanced, star-faring civilization — and went over to Earth to introduce themselves.

In the film, the overly aggressive Borg collective travels back in time to stop Cochrane from making that first flight. The Enterprise chases them back in time to make sure the Borg fails, and the closing scene shows Cochrane and the Vulcans meeting each other.

I'm a sucker for these first-contact movies that revolve around humans and aliens interacting with essentially peaceful motivations.

I'm sure there are earlier examples, but I'd start with the original version of *The Day The Earth Stood Still* (1951), where Klaatu and his robot Gort attempt to present Earth with a device that would enable us to study life on other planets, until a trigger-happy government employee pumps a round into him. Klaatu ends up becoming a world cop, leaving Gort behind to prevent further bloodshed, so it's not exactly a happy ending. More satisfying endings happen in:

It Came From Outer Space (1953), in which aliens crash-land and do some body snatching, but only so they can fix their boat. Otherwise they have come in peace.

2001: A Space Odyssey (1968) and its more literal sequel, *2010: The Year We Make Contact,* in which we never really meet the aliens but their mission is clearly to help us evolve to the next, more noble, stage.

Close Encounters of the Third Kind (1977), in which, when we finally meet the mysterious aliens, our hero joyously rides off with them in an apparent mission to explore strange new worlds and new civilizations.

E.T. The Extra-Terrestrial (1982), in which an alien botanist gets stranded on Earth and befriends a little boy. This sweet story is one of my all-time favorite films and, tangentially, the John Williams soundtrack is that fine composer's finest hour, er, two hours.

Contact (1997), a cross between the secretive aliens of *2001* and the *Close Encounters* aliens who invite us humans along for the intergalactic ride, albeit using small moves, Ellie.

And finally, *Arrival* (2016), a magnificent film and my favorite of the 21st century so far, in which a dedicated linguistics professor races to translate the language and culture of visiting aliens before we paranoid humans can blow them (and ourselves) up. Once again, their goal is meaningful communication but some of us can't get over our fears.

What these movies have in common is the notion that aliens among us generally have nonviolent and benevolent intent, and our fears and prejudices make us act in unwelcome ways that hinder the process at best and make us the true villains of the story at worst.

If we dig deep enough, we almost always find that we have more in common than differences. I would rather be the foolish scientist who tries to reason with the alien and gets swatted away than the kid who shoots the benevolent stranger out of fear. Of course, my real preference is to be Elliot helping E.T. get home, or Ellie making small moves on the beach with the image of her father, or Roy Neary signing up to fly into space, or Louise Banks figuring out what Abbott and Costello have been trying to say.

I would suggest these stories intend to encourage us to be willing to embrace the strange and the unknown and find a common understanding to move forward together. That's why I regard these movies with more fondness than, say, *War of the Worlds* (1953) or *Independence Day* (1996), which are tremendous stories in their own right but present the aliens as would-be conquerors. I think the films I've listed here have a healthier outlook.

Comfort while the storm rages

One of my favorite photos is a picture taken behind one of our golden retrievers, who was sitting quietly at the window while a snowstorm raged outside. I posted the photo online one morning with the caption, "Peace can be having nothing to do except watch the dogs watching the snow fall." I got more than my share of "amens." I stretched the truth, of course — I had things to do; I just was just letting some of them slide.

Those of us not far from the waters of Green Bay, Wisconsin, were finally getting assaulted by winter. A week ago there had been no snow on the ground — almost unheard of in these parts during the first week in January — and in a matter of days we had close to a foot. We did not have a White Christmas, but that has changed dramatically starting around the 13th Day of Christmas.

When the infrastructure is working, it is peaceful to look out the window and watch nature at work. Wisconsin Public Service Corp. continues to deliver a reliable energy flow, the propane company keeps my heating supply topped off, and the indoor plumbing is working like a charm. I see the birds gathered around the feeder and feel bad for them — my little supply of seed is their only modern convenience against the raging storm. And that brings to mind the humans who are not as fortunate as I am.

A winter storm a few years ago knocked out power for about two weeks to the home where my father and brother were living in New Jersey, a place most folks probably consider more civilized than rural Wisconsin. Bad stuff can happen anywhere and anytime; it's kind of scary to think so, but there it is.

We owe it to each other to take care of each

other. I'm not talking about government programs and some imagined duty to pay taxes so well-fed bureaucrats can redistribute a fraction of what has been seized from everyday folks; I'm talking about everyday folks sharing what they can to help their neighbors when it's needed. The funny thing is when the chips are down, they always manage to share what they can. A few days after the storm, our local United Way announced that they raised the most they ever raised, despite the less than stellar economy we're struggling through, and many churches have Helping Hands Funds to take care of folks who need caring for.

Peace can be having nothing to do except watch the dogs watching the snow fall. Peace is also something that humans give each other. I dare say the natural state of humans is peace on Earth, if only the war mongers would shut up and go home.

End the stupid

I never heard the expression "I know you are, but what am I?" until (of all things) the movie *Pee Wee's Big Adventure*.

It comes to mind as I watch the reaction to the new song "Try That in a Small Town," which suggests that big-city violence would not have a long shelf life in a smaller community.

"See how far ya make it down the road; Around here, we take care of our own," sings Jason Aldean. "You cross that line, it won't take long for you to find out."

The reaction went something like this: "That song is racist!" "I know you are, but what am I? Your songs advocate violence, too! You're the racist!" "I know you are, but what am I?"

It's stupid to condone violence under any

circumstances. It's stupid to make judgments based on race or skin color under any circumstances. And what is "race" if not separation based on skin color? We're all *homo sapiens* — all this talk about different human races is a silly (or evil) attempt to divide and perhaps (probably) conquer.

It all comes down to a single law — Love one another, one of two central laws — the other is Love God.

All this noise — all these screams of "You started it!" and "I'm just responding to what you said/did" — is a variation on "I know you are, but what am I?" Enough already. Can we just get back to Love God and Love one another? And if you can't wrap your mind around God, can we at least try loving one another? Do you have a problem with love? Really?

The cycle of violence/retaliation ends either when someone refuses to retaliate or when everyone's dead. Myself, I prefer the idea of someone refusing to meet violence with violence. Peace has to start somewhere, with someone.

Maybe we can live as God intended

I never heard "Dear Ivan" until Saturday, when the SiriusXM '60s channel played the Top 40 songs from Jan. 20, 1962. That was the week "Dear Ivan" peaked at #24.

Jimmy Dean had had a monster hit a couple months earlier with "Big Bad John," and he followed up with another talking song that is a letter to a Soviet farmer from himself, an American former farmer.

At the height of the Cold War — smack between the establishment of the Berlin Wall and the Cuban Missile Crisis — Dean writes to the Russian, "I'd like to walk up and shake your hand and look you straight in the eye and tell you that I haven't got one thing in this world against you.

"I know that the heads of our government seem to have problems getting together to talk things over, but I got a feeling if you and I could just sit down and talk not as representatives of anybody's government but just two plain ordinary human beings, I feel that we might think a great deal alike."

I listened in shock as Jimmy Dean talked about how the Russians and Americans fought on the same side against the Nazis just a few years earlier, and that he figures they both still would like to see "a world united in peace."

He wrote this at the end of 1961, when the war mongers were hard at work fomenting hatred against Russians and looking for excuses to bomb America's foes into the Stone Age. And here's the guy who had the #2 song in the country a few weeks before, suggesting that the "evil Russkies" were human beings just like us and that recognizing each other's humanity is bigger than any differences their governments might have.

"Ivan, when I put my babies to bed tonight, I'm gonna say a prayer for you and yours, and if you in your own way will say a prayer for me and mine, and maybe we can talk our neighbors into doing the same thing, this will be more powerful than any conference held over any conference table anywhere in the whole wide world, and then maybe we can live as God intended — peacefully, together."

It's one thing for me, after 62 years of increasing skepticism about whether government and the advocates of never-ending war can be trusted, to call for an end to the madness and recognize that normal human beings want to live in peace with other human beings, not blow them up.

I salute Jimmy Dean for having the courage to say it with the Cold War raging. It speaks volumes that 62 years went by before I heard the song. This is not a sentiment The Powers That Be want shared, even now.

It starts with the first to say 'no'

I have been spending a great deal of words lately calling for an end to mass murder as a legitimate response to conflict in a civilized society. As John Lennon wrote in his famous Christmas song, "War is over if you want it."

Of course, I know it's not that simple. We're not going to agree to end war and live happily ever after, as if, "Let's stop killing each other — you go first."

It's a complicated question and there are no easy answers. I understand that.

And yet —

Jeanette Rankin was the first woman to serve in the U.S. House of Representatives. The voters of Montana elected her to two terms 24 years apart, and she served 1917-1919 and 1941-1943.

In 1917, Rankin was one was one of 50 representatives and six senators who voted against sending the U.S. military into the Great War. In 1941, she was the only member of Congress to vote against declaring war against Japan after the Pearl Harbor attack.

Long, long before I wrote it, Rankin said war "is a wrong method of trying to settle a dispute."

Her first vote came at a time when women could not go to war and were not even allowed to vote in elections. "As a woman I can't go to war, and I refuse to send anyone else," she said, and, "I felt the first time the first woman had a chance to say no to war, she should say it."

Someone does have to be the first to go first, to give an example and inspire the one who goes second, and third, and eventually hundreds and thousands and millions and, we must hope, billions.

Someday we may solve our differences with words and not violence, certainly not mass murder, but that day will only come if someone like Jeanette

Rankin steps forward and says, "No. We do not kill our enemies. Mass murder is never justified, even if we dress it up in pretty clothes and call it something else, like war."

It's not that simple, but really, it is that simple. War is not a sane answer to any question.

The words must be there, somewhere

I am a bit of an introvert, and the blog is my way of reaching out to communicate with the outside world. "This is what I'm thinking; how about you?"

Words are marvelous inventions that allow us to share our minds one with another. Where are the words, though, that will lead us at last to understanding?

We can speak to each other face to face across thousands of miles and see the creases around each other's eyes. Words give us access to the minds of people who died centuries ago. Our technology of communication is unfathomable compared with 100, 200, and 300 years ago.

And we don't communicate well why?

The words are there. The intentions, I think, are there. Who wants to live in war and fear of violence? Who would want to impose war and violence on others?

"Ah," one might reply, "but it is a violent world. Just look at nature." No, I don't believe that violent men are mimicking nature. If the universe tends to entropy and inertia, after all — Damn, this thought is not forming properly, perhaps because I just can't understand why, if people want peace, peace proves elusive.

Maybe if you place seven — eight now? — billion souls, each with a unique outlook and needs and desires, on one large orb, then clashes are inevitable.

And yet, we just need to agree to live and let live … and maybe that's the problem. Maybe the "and let live" part gets in the way.

People don't want to let people live in certain ways or with certain beliefs, and so there is no peace. Other people want to force everyone to live the way they do, and so there is no peace.

But a guy can dream.

Free people seek the light, always

I wish I could remember where I saw it, and I wish I had written it down, or saved it, or printed it out, but I don't and I didn't so ...

You'll just have to take my word for it. (You do remember when a person's word was his/her bond, right?)

Some time back I read about a historian who had tracked civilization's ups and downs in waves, and this person predicted that the next great downward wave, a downturn bordering on dark ages, would begin in 2020.

I think about that article lately.

But it's in my nature to seek the light.

I am so glad to live in a land where people drafted a Bill of Rights to restrict bad people from doing bad things, tyrannical things, to everyday people. Even though they still do bad things, tyrannical things, at least there's a standard against which those things can be judged bad.

When the age looks very dark, that's a very dim light to hang my hat on, I know. Barely a candle's flicker on a breezy day.

Many of my favorite works of fiction are dystopian: *Nineteen Eighty-Four*, of course, and *Animal Farm*, and the 1960s TV show *The Prisoner* with its iconic shout of defiance: "I am not a number, I am a free man!"

Notice that: Held captive in a Village where faceless rulers insist that everyone think and act the same, where contrary thought is punished and no one may leave, this person cries, "I am a free man!"

And he is.

And, as darkness appears to be falling, and bad people are attempting to shepherd everyone into sheepish little villages and silence everyone who doesn't think or act correctly, that flicker refuses to be extinguished.

We are free. Many don't quite understand, but

that's The Thing about freedom: We are "endowed at birth" with it, so it's always ours to exercise or surrender.

Bullies love to try forcing free people to surrender, but we keep reading and collecting the banned books, gathering in groups or retreating in solitary to speak and write what we please, creating great art and great businesses that free the mind, body and soul.

The response to tyranny's violence is not more violence, because that plays into the bully's hands. The bully can only tear down; the free person builds, always. No, the response is simply to be free. The tyrant needs your permission to take your freedom, and you needn't give it.

If a new dark age is starting, then we protect the light. Every warming campfire begins with a flicker.

Good for nothing

Try as I might, I can't think of a reason to kill you. That is to say, I can't think of circumstances that would justify taking the life of another human being.

I suppose if you were to attack me with deadly force and it was a case of kill or be killed ... but even then I'd like to think I'd try to defend myself with something less than lethal.

War is just about the most foolish institution humans have ever concocted. As the song says, "What is it good for? Absolutely nothing!"

War doesn't convince your enemies to see it your way. If anything, war creates more enemies in the form of people who had no quarrel with you who have lost friends and family at your hands.

You can raise money for fighting and killing and to make sure the other damn fool dies for his country, as General Patton once said, if that's what you like. Me, I'm going to lay down my sword and shield down by the riverside and study war no more.

Mother's Day Proclamation

Julia Ward Howe, also known for writing "Battle Hymn of the Republic," wrote this proclamation in 1870.

Here we are, 154 years later, and the pain and the sentiment are still relevant.

It's possible that, 154 years from now, nothing will have changed.

But we have to try.

+ + + + +

Arise, then, women of this day! Arise all women who have hearts, whether your baptism be that of water or of fears! Say firmly: "We will not have great questions decided by irrelevant agencies, our husbands shall not come to us, reeking with carnage, for caresses and applause. "Our sons shall not be taken from us to unlearn all that we have been to teach them of charity, mercy, and patience. We women of one country will be too tender of those of another country to allow our sons to be trained to injure theirs." From the bosom of the devastated earth a voice goes up with our own. It says, "Disarm, Disarm!The sword of murder is not the balance of justice." Blood does not wipe out dishonor nor violence indicate possession. As men have often forsaken the plow and the anvil at the summons of war, let women now leave all that may be left of home for a great and earnest day of counsel. Let them meet first, as women, to bewail and commemorate the dead. Let them then solemnly take counsel with each other as the means whereby the great human family can live in peace, and each bearing after her own time the sacred impress, not of Caesar, but of God. In the name of womanhood and of humanity, I earnestly ask that a general congress of women without limit of nationality may be appointed and held at some place deemed most convenient and at the earliest period consistent with its objects, to promote the alliance of the different nationalities, the amicable settlement of international questions, the great and general interests of peace.

— Julia Ward Howe

Part 3

Who Will Stand For Peace?

100 A DECLARATION OF PEACE

A way out of the mess

We toiled for years under the illusion that the leaders of the U.S. government were good humans who wanted to preserve ideals of truth, justice, and liberty. Was it ever so? It certainly is not now.

The presidential candidates over the past 32 years have all either been very wealthy to begin with or slick con men who used the tools of politics and government to make themselves wealthy — and once wealth insulates you from the concerns of everyday humans, it's easy to tax them into slavery and bully them into any sort of ghastly behavior, from waging war against strangers to submitting to bizarre medical experiments.

The U.S. government is a pathetic shadow parroting Jefferson's Declaration of Independence but refusing to live by even a shred of its meaning. In the absence of decency, the least we can do is refuse to participate in the charade. At a minimum I won't vote for these people.

So much of this mess is out of the everyday human's control that it seems hopeless to preserve truth, justice or liberty, but even the bloated and corrupt leviathan cannot be everywhere. What we CAN do is use what resources are left to us to be kind in the face of bullies, to live our lives as if we are free — that is to say, to be a living example of what a true and decent human looks like, living in peace and loving our neighbors.

I hesitate to mention the name of Jesus because that name has been misused and misrepresented by petty tyrants and narrow-minded bigots down through the ages, but Jesus and his apostles are the best example I have for what I mean. These were people who lives by the essential laws of love God and love your neighbors. These were people who believed that "the fruit of the spirit is love, joy, peace, forbearance, kindness, goodness, faithfulness, gentleness, and self-control. Against such things there is no law." (Galatians 5:22-23)

Could we really build a peaceful world on that

gentle but firm foundation? Why not? The bullies would howl and belittle the followers of such a path, and probably even maim and kill as many as they felt they could get away with — but they have a basic flaw, and that is their way of thinking is wrong, detrimental to humanity, and, well, simply indecent.

The bloated leviathan someday will collapse upon itself, and what is left could be as brutal and lawless as the leviathan itself — or it could be grounded in the fruit of the spirit, if we start building that gentle but firm foundation, today.

No more bullies

When we are young, we are taught that the playground bully is wrong.

Adults punish the child who is caught pummeling his victims into submission.

Then we grow up and follow the bullies who enforce their will by means of greater weaponry.

The rule is that whoever kills the most others is the winner.

No more, we say.

Pummeling the most playground victims is not leadership.

It's time to wage peace on this world.

Subdue your adversaries with kindness.

See no human as your enemy, only as your neighbor.

And love your neighbors.

Live, and love.

In peace.

The goal
of most sane humans

The laptop is in my lap, I am sitting in our love seat, and Summer has curled up next to me with her head against my hip, so I have to extend my right arm to manipulate the keys. It is much more comfortable to pull my arm down and pet her head and stroke her fur; I have little doubt she planned it that way.

Tonight the supposed leader of the free world gave his State of the Union address. Even though I work in the news business, I haven't watched this speech for years. It's all about fighting — fighting his political adversaries, fighting for some imagined agenda, fighting about whatever country he is sending kids to fight in, always fighting, except when he pauses to use people as props, people who were invited to sit in the balcony and smile and wave while the president praises them and thanks them for whatever it was that earned them that seat.

No, thank you. I've heard enough States of the Union with their calls to the war *du jour*. I would rather sit with a sleeping golden retriever and think about peace.

You remember peace, the natural state of things, the goal of most sane humans.

We have so much more in common with our neighbors than any differences that the petty demagogues and sociopaths drum up, but demagogues and sociopaths can be charming, as you know, and before you know it they have you whipped into a frenzied anger because how could those other people be so ... so ... so ... well, they're so whatever my favorite sociopath says they are, and what are we going to do about it!

You can play the shouting game all you like. It's a shame that we let the nasties get under our skin so much. Most of the time humans get along — we live and love and do business and play together in peace. The anomalies become news stories because they are anomalies — the person who lashed out in anger, the plane that didn't land safely, the honest person victimized by a thief — but because the anomalies are broadcast far and wide, we start to believe hatred and violence and crime are commonplace.

People want peace; it's as simple as that. I don't want to pick a fight, and neither do you. Tell me you'd rather be pushing and shoving than sitting in a love seat snuggled with a golden retriever — or whatever your vision of a perfectly peaceful moment is — and I'll smile, think about calling you a liar, then think twice because I just said I don't want to pick a fight.

Nope, I just want to sit here and watch this beautiful dog sleep.

Memorial Day: No more war

We set aside the fourth Monday in May each year to honor and remember the people who have died in war. From time to time someone points out that the best way to honor war dead is to work to ensure there is no war.

But war goes on, and perhaps it always will as long as we turn for leadership to disturbed people who would violently take land from and kill those they perceive as enemies.

Life is a precious gift, too precious to leave in the hands of death merchants. To honor the victims of war, may we raise a chorus of "Never again. May we resolve our future differences in peace."

The greatest laws

I keep coming back to the last thing I read to Red as she made the transition to the next world, which is the most concise mission statement a Christian could hope for:

The greatest commandment, Jesus said, is "'You shall love the Lord your God with all your heart and with all your soul and with all your mind.' This is the great and first commandment. And a second is like it: 'You shall love your neighbor as yourself.' On these two commandments depend all the Law and the Prophets."

Meanwhile, my political philosophy boils down to what has been dubbed the Zero Aggression Principle, which is not unlike the two greatest commandments: "No one has the right, under any circumstances, to initiate force against another human being for any reason whatever, nor advocate the initiation of force, or delegate it to anyone else."

It occurs to me that these statements are all about how to interact with other people, person to person. Treat other people with love, and don't initiate violence against anyone.

Person to person, I think most people have no problem treating other people with love, or at least respect. If you think through the average day, you have dozens of peaceful, nonviolent interactions with other people.

Things start going awry when we remove that personal interaction from the equation. Road rage is between two people separated by tons of steel at high speed. Online bullying is, of course, not face-to-face. Racial and ethnic violence is the opposite of treating people as individuals.

The most active agent of initiating force, of course, is government. The average state is a blunt force instrument, and politicians as a general rule treat each other and the average citizen with anything but love.

I wonder how much easier it would be to love one another, and live in peace with our neighbors, if we didn't have politicians and other agents of the state on our shoulders whispering (or shouting) violent words of hate all the time.

I can't think of a better mission statement. Yes, yes, I know, not everyone believes in God, let alone loves God, but can we agree that a love for something bigger than ourselves is a key to a healthier life? And I know people have done awful things professing a love for God, but that's their fault, not God's.

And that second commandment: "Love your neighbor as yourself." Recognize your neighbor's humanity and worth, and recognize that everyone is your neighbor on this big little planet of ours.

Can you imagine how much better our lives could be if we all followed these commandments?

We could get along if we wanted

Sometimes I think about how any number of things may have unfolded differently in my youth had I had the ability to call or send a message/text at a key moment.

Think how many classic stories would be ruined if they were set in the modern era — stories where something tragic happens because of not being able to communicate, say if Romeo or Juliet had been able to send a text saying, "Don't be alarmed, I'm going to try something, it's not what it looks like."

We have in the palm of our hand, the ability to reach across the miles and avoid all sorts of catastrophes and misunderstandings in a way that was unfathomable when many of us were younger. We are linked. We can connect at a moment's notice to anyone almost anywhere on the planet.

And yet the same catastrophes and misunderstandings keep happening.

It seems the ability to communicate is not the same as the will to communicate.

A day for bridge building

And what kind of a day shall this be? Meteorologists spend hours poring over the signs to determine how the atmosphere may behave today, and so we have some sense of what kind of day it will be in terms of sun or rain or wind or calm or storms or all of the above — but what kind of a day shall this be?

There is much that is not mine to control — some of it is up to the whims of the animals who live with me under this roof. Other factors are the people I will interact with today — what is on their mind, and how can I make it easier for them? How can I remind them of the good in this world, how can I help them during the brief moments or minutes or hours that I will be a part of their day?

If I am to be just a passing glance of an

encounter, then so be it, but if I am able to leave an impression, let it be one that builds bridges and a sense of relief that life is worth the effort and we are in this together. Keep anger far from my soul and banish hatred altogether — place patience and love on my lips that I may spread them far and near.

May I practice loving my neighbor so well and so often that it comes as naturally as it does to a musician who has devoted 10,000 hours to her instrument. Let today be one of those days, and may I remember to frame tomorrow and tomorrow with even greater love.

There's a catch

There's a catch in the Lord's Prayer.

It says "Forgive us our sins *as we forgive those who sin against us.*"

The same kind of catch is in one of the two great laws.

It says "Love your neighbor *as yourself.*"

We're praying that God forgive our sins only to the extent that we forgive those who sin against us. And if we have no self-respect, we're going to have trouble loving our neighbors.

Do unto others as you would have them do unto you. The first move's on you; that is to say, it's up to us.

Beatitudes

Jesus' Sermon on the Mount launches with eight pretty powerful blessings. As quoted in the Gospel of Matthew, they are:

Blessed are the poor in spirit, for theirs is the kingdom of heaven.

Blessed are those who mourn, for they will be comforted.

Blessed are the meek, for they will inherit the earth.

Blessed are those who hunger and thirst for righteousness, for they will be filled.

Blessed are the merciful, for they will be shown mercy.

Blessed are the pure in heart, for they will see

God.

Blessed are the peacemakers, for they will be called sons of God.

Blessed are those who are persecuted because of righteousness, for theirs is the kingdom of heaven.

(I never understood who the "poor in spirit" are supposed to be, but I learned tonight it's folks who recognize they need God. That makes sense in context.)

The people who were listening had to be a little confused by some of this. All right, let's understand that we need God and we should hunger and thirst to be righteous and pure in heart. But what's this stuff about being meek and merciful and peacemakers?

Shouldn't a God-fearing person be strong and forceful about proclaiming and enforcing God's laws? And this bit a little later when he says if somebody slaps you in the face, you should offer up the other side of your face so he can slap that, too? Wait just a cotton-picking minute.

Jesus here is serving up the recipe for non-violent civil disobedience that the likes of Gandhi and Martin Luther King finally embraced during the 20th century. Yep, it took nearly 2,000 years of religious leaders going to war and forcing Christianity on reluctant and/or conquered souls before somebody took to heart what Jesus was trying to say here.

Jesus, Gandhi and King were all assassinated. That's how dangerous non-violence is to some people. Make peace? Be humble of heart and, for crying out loud, merciful? That sort of talk needs to be put down, and hard.

This life Jesus was talking about was not easy — the gentle and the loving tend to be ground up and spit out in what passes for "real life" in this day and age. But imagine how much better this world could be if we took these words to heart.

No time for hate

In the quiet of morning, when thoughts are free to surface without the clamor of everything else, the needs of the day seem manageable and ordered. Emotions are free to wash over me without interruption or fear of discovery. The blessings are clear, and the losses cut as deeply as they require. Everything is waiting on up ahead.

The day emerges slowly with the sun, and there is time for everything — a time to rejoice, a time to mourn, a time for love, and wait a minute: Must there really be a time for hate? What do we gain except bitter almond when we give hate our time of day?

The Old Testament poet said there is a time for love, a time for hate, a time for war, a time for peace. But the New Testament savior said it's all wrapped up in Love God and Love One Another. Is there really a time for hate, or a time for war, if our mission is Love?

Oh, I don't deny that men and women squabble and fight and otherwise overlook how little time we have for such nonsense. And 7 billion people will have 7 billion understandings of what Love is and how to express Love. One person's words of love may be another person's hate speech, and vice versa. Is conflict inevitable? Conflict is the stuff of literature and adventure and a great love story. But hate? But war? These are signs of sickness, and the goal with any illness is to heal, to find a cure, to eradicate the disease if we can.

In the still of the morning, it seems so simple to inject love into every transaction. But it does seem inevitable that the day ahead will bring a flash of anger, outrage, incomprehension, ugliness, and there will be the hatred and the rumors of war again in all their glory. Perhaps the best we can accomplish is the effort, to try to love, to try to keep in mind what is, after all, a concept of only six words: Love God and Love One Another. Of course, some will argue whether God even exists and dismiss the notion altogether, and others will argue that some people are not worthy of our love, but the nature of real love is that there are no conditions.

Sure as Judas betrayed Jesus, I feel certain that I will betray the mission of Love sometime during the day ahead, sadly enough, but is there a better goal than to Love God and Love One Another as best I can? Can I harm my neighbor by approaching her with love? Can I hurt my neighbor by treating him with love?

And from a selfish standpoint, being patient and kind and keeping no record of wrongs and the like is easier on my soul. If I relinquish the bile, I relax the tension in my body.

The day begins to press in, but perhaps this reflection will linger for a while and underline my interactions, and maybe a spirit of love can spread through me to the next person down the line, and that will be a start. At the very least, it's worth a try.

The myth of the masses

There was an empire and an emperor, and neither could see faces; they only saw the people, and they treated the people as if they were their children, and they taught the people to serve the emperor and the empire, but they never saw the faces, they only saw the mass, and they didn't see that inside that mass were infinite numbers of faces, and many were hurting, and many suffered.

But one day, a person stood up and said, "I have an idea." And another called back, "I've had that idea, too." And others said, "Yes, and here's another idea." And all of them had faces. That was how it began, you see: That was how people began to stop thinking of themselves as "the masses" and began to see each other.

They realized that there was no single,

amorphous mass, only a great number of individuals with the ability to work together in harmony, each of them so powerful that a proverb said, "When an old person dies, a library burns to the ground." When they understood that the true power resides inside each individual, the false and manufactured power of the empire began to fade, until it came to pass that everyone understood the emperor was simply another individual, no greater or lesser than any other of us.

Darkness descends, and night may last a very long time, but some of us remember and whisper about the light and the promise and the face of hope. That may not be much, but some day it will be enough.

I am not your enemy

I wander onto social media and see all these memes designed to provoke and divide us, and I wonder why some people are so intent on splitting us into warring camps.

The memes contain the essence of one political party's talking points with the implication that to disagree is to believe the extreme opposite in the cruelest sense. You know the sort of thing: "I belong to my party because I don't believe kittens deserve to be eaten."

Every couple of years in the U.S., a professional pig wrestling tournament is held — some call it an election — in which the participants are cast in terms of good and evil, honest and corrupt, noble and ignoble, and once the wrestling is over, the expectation is that the winners are to go into a room and cooperate to solve all our problems. The thing is, if they believe what they were saying about each other, how can they possibly work together? And sure enough, the ensuing conversations are little more than a continuation of the pig-wrestling campaign.

And now so many people are caught up in this belief that one political party or another is the sole champion of truth and justice and morality, and if you don't swallow every tenet you surely are a spawn or a pawn of Satan, or at least of Russia or China.

Don't get me wrong. Folks are free to say and believe what they want, and I don't want anyone to police or censor "hateful speech" on social media. For one thing, reasonable people disagree over what hate speech actually is. You may see a passionate defense of your political party while all I can see is your hate seething from the page, and vice versa.

I just suggest that you put yourself in the shoes of your opponent and consider that they seek a path to truth and justice that's simply different from yours, not evil. No one is opposed to truth or justice, except perhaps someone who benefits from pitting humans against each other. Who do you suppose that might be, and why would they want to do that?

Wage peace

I am not the first, nor will I be the last, to suggest the phrase "wage peace" as a counter to waging war. A commitment to resolving conflict nonviolently is surely more difficult than waging war and therefore deserves the same verb — "wage."

After all, the primordial instinct to punch you in the face is easier than explaining to you how wrong I think you are and that I intend to stop you from proceeding by any means possible short of killing or maiming you and your followers.

At least it sounds difficult. As a matter of fact, we wage peace every day as we go about our lives. The vast majority of us today will not commit violence or crimes against any of our fellow humans, let alone wage war, a crime against humanity itself.

"It's human nature," some will say, "you will never eradicate war from the earth." You're probably right, and maybe I will never finish that challenge, but I can nibble at the edges and get the job started for others to finish when I am gone.

Jesus got the ball rolling when he said, "Love your neighbor as yourself." Treat your fellow human with the same kindness and respect you hope to be afforded yourself. Sure you do not wish to be killed or maimed, and so make a commitment not to kill or maim your neighbor. The idea sounds ridiculous when you're talking about your next-door neighbor, but every victim of war is somebody's next-door neighbor, isn't she? Isn't he? Aren't they?

This morning I feel like sharing blessings and benedictions this morning, but they don't get past the first words — "May the God of ..." or "May God who ..."

It feels like a time to send encouragement and optimism into the world. The words teeter at the edge of my mind as if it were the tip of my tongue, as if mere words could solve the woes that threaten to sink beleaguered souls.

I believe in mere words, though. I believe those old saws about the pen being mightier than the sword — the metaphor does have more power than cold steel. You might end my life prematurely with your dastardly weapon, but my words have already escaped and flown here and there, and maybe only a few have seen or heard them, but one or more might shape them better than I did into words that will convince many more, and my influence will save more lives than your rusty sword ever ended.

"Oh, he pretends to be an influencer now, does he?" you scoff as the blade does its business.

We are all "influencers." We touch other lives every time we walk out the door — and those of us who share our homes don't even need to do that. We touch other lives as we drive down the highway, gather groceries at the store, toil at our workplaces, cheer at the ballgame, and otherwise live our lives. A kind word or a rude gesture touch other lives, as do a smile or a blank stare.

Influencers are all around us, and none more

important than the one we see in the mirror.

Our words pave the highway, or the rambling country road, that our future will travel. Our words are the fuel that nourishes our family, friends and colleagues and neighbors and strangers. Our words can be seeds of encouragement and comfort, or we can sow hatred and dissension, and either choice can spread far and wide. We choose moment by moment which future we will conjure, with our words and accompanying actions.

And there is the blessing and benediction I sought — May the God of the universe give you words today that will lead us all to peace.

Will anyone stand for peace?

My friend texted me with news of strife on U.S. campuses, knowing I don't watch the morning news.

Here is a generation taking sides in an ancient hatred — choosing sides in an exchange of mass murder, as if one side or another in an exchange of mass murder could ever be righteous.

My generation at least had some people who protested the very idea of mass murder as a legitimate institution.

Remember the anti-war movement? Its symbols were the peace sign and the photo of the girl placing a flower in the barrel of a soldier's rifle.

This generation, born after 9/11, has grown up in a surveillance state where hatred is part of everyday life. Now coming of age, they are deciding whom to hate. All individuals are lumped into groups, and the hate is directed at those groups to save the trouble of getting to know the individuals.

Will anyone stand for peace?

We are awash with proclamations — "I stand with Israel. I stand with Ukraine. I stand with Gaza. I stand with You Name The Place Where People Are Killing and Being Killed."

Will anyone stand for peace?

Where is this generation's Mahatma Gandhi or Rev. King who will stand for a peaceful and nonviolent resolution? Where has reason fled? Where is "Love Your Neighbor"?

Where is the girl with the flower?

This world is weary of hate, division, violence, bombs and guns to settle our differences, body bags, and politicians with blood on their hands offering up political "solutions" that betray freedom and cause even more division.

Surely there is a voice, somewhere in this wilderness, crying out for peace. I swear I hear a

134 A DECLARATION OF PEACE

vast throng crying for an end to the madness and an end to the killing.

But ...

Will anyone stand for peace?

Author's note

So there is my collection of thoughts on war, peace, and nonviolent ways to resolve our differences. You might say I'm a dreamer, but I'm not the only one, as a singer once sang.

Who am I, anyway? Just a kid from New Jersey who was just a little too young to fight in the Vietnam War. The war actually was still on when I reached drafting age, but it was the year they instituted a draft "lottery" — if your birthday was drawn first, you went to the front of the line. My birthday was drawn some distance after 300.

I went to Wisconsin to attend Ripon College, starting a year after the anti-war protests flared up and died out on college campuses. At every step where I might have taken a stand for peace, I didn't really have to anymore.

I never got over the idea that war was stupid, however. The thoughts I expressed in my blog posts, and collected in this book, had been simmering for decades before I finally started voicing them. I feel a bit foolish for waiting all those decades.

Be that as it may, where do we go from here? I suspect I will leave this mortal coil in a few years, give or take, and very little will have changed. Insane people — some of them masquerading as statesmen — will continue to commit mass murder, and their angry victims will lash back in kind, goaded by other insane people, some of them masquerading as statesmen.

At least I have taken the time to point out that this behavior is uncivilized, insane, and worse than senseless, and you have taken the time to read and digest these thoughts. Maybe between the two of us, we can begin the long, tedious task of changing minds around the world so that eventually life will be recognized as too valuable to throw away in this manner.

I'm not much of a praying man, but when I do pray, I pray for peace. May God have mercy on our souls.

Warren Bluhm

May 2024

May we live without destruction

May we look to tomorrow with hope

May peace and light return to us

Milton Keynes UK
Ingram Content Group UK Ltd.
UKHW020125021224
451695UK00019B/289